SUNDAY EXPRESS AND

DAILY EXPRESS

CARTOONS

4/6

MADE AND PRINTED IN GREAT BRITAIN BY GREYCAINES
(TAYLOR GARNETT EVANS & CO LTD.), WATFORD, HERTS.

Original edition published 1947.
This Facsimile edition printed in Italy
and published under licence by Pedigree Books Limited.
Giles Characters™ and ©1995 Express Newspapers plc.

SUNDAY EXPRESS & DAILY EXPRESS
CARTOONS

Second Series

Published by
LANE PUBLICATIONS LTD.

by ARTHUR CHRISTIANSEN

Editor-in-Chief of the Daily Express

I HAVE only one thing against Giles—he will not work in London. Ever since he joined the *Express* organisation he has firmly and successfully resisted my attempts to persuade him to leave his studios in Ipswich.

I see him only once a month on average. For the rest my business is conducted by telephone. And Giles in turn telephones to say that his cartoon has been despatched by a train that will eventually arrive at Liverpool Street Station.

You will see, therefore, that I have no hand in the creation of a Giles cartoon. Editors are able to guide and assist many of their contributors, and like the Russians have the right to say "No". But Giles has his own operational methods. He is a law unto himself. I usually say "Yes".

And, with the growth of experience in nursing this extraordinary man, I am bound to admit that he is right to shun London. For his genius derives from contact with the people. Not the people of Fleet Street who on the whole are an odd and peculiar tribe, but the simple, solid people who live simple, solid lives and are the backbone of Britain.

Giles interprets their moods, their humour, their reaction to great events. He views Whitehall and Westminster as a distant scene and keeps his perspective true by avoiding close contact with the know-alls, the V.I.P.'s and the people who think they are V.I.P.'s.

My colleague John Gordon, editor of the *Sunday Express*, introduced the Giles cartoon book last year. He then made the comment that if you look at people closely as they pass by in the street you will find they are Giles characters. I must repeat his view and give it my support, because I believe it to be the secret of the man.

Giles does not caricature. He does not fake. He does not invent. He draws real buildings, real pubs, real railway stations, as anyone who knows East Anglia and travels L.N.E.R. will realise.

And he draws from the largest and finest selection of models that any artist could wish—the British people.

I commend Giles to them with confidence and with great respect.

Arthur Christiansen

"You can come out now, Grandma—they're not going to drop any more bombs for a long time."

Daily Express, July 2nd, 1946

"When I think of their rationing, their income tax, and all the dough we're going to take off them today—my heart bleeds for them, Alf—bleeds for them."

Daily Express, June 5th, 1946

"Sit still, Sidney—you'll 'ave the blooming lot over."

Daily Express, June 7th, 1946

"I've queued for me fish, me bread and me vegetables—now for me Victory stamps."

Daily Express, June 13th, 1946

"Remember, men—no premature celebrations.   Wait till it's definite."

Daily Express, June 18th, 1946

"It didn't take 40,000 men, 200 goats, 200 pigs and 3,000 rats to test one good old-fashioned cannon ball."

Daily Express, June 26th, 1946

Opportunities missed cannot be repeated.

Daily Express, June 27th, 1946

"Now don't forget—anyone hanging around with a wistful look in their eye—let 'em have it—bing, bang!"

Daily Express, July 4th, 1946

Daily Express, July 11th, 1946

"Just in case petrol comes off the ration, in future we will assume that possibly the customer may be sometimes right."

Sunday Express, July 14th, 1946

"Remember, men—if you want the beer to last out for the rest of the week, make every shot count."

Daily Express, July 16th, 1946

"Scram, boys—the cops!"

Daily Express, July 18th, 1946

"They'll soon take that silly grin off their faces when you explain to them about our British rationing."
A new consignment of animals has just arrived at the London Zoo.

Sunday Express, July 21st, 1946

"You know your stuff; soon as this fella's corn's ready for cutting, Spike and Eddie go in with the binder—
Spider and the boys give 'em covering fire if necessary."

Daily Express, July 25th, 1946

"Jenkins, I suppose there isn't even the remotest possibility of tapping Cook for one small crust for bread bait?"

Sunday Express, July 28th, 1946

"Hooray! Someone's pinched the car! Now I shan't have to take the family to the —— seaside for the week-end."

Daily Express, Aug. 1st, 1946

"Don't be silly—sitting there fretting in case Mr. Morrison has a go at your favourite comic while we're away."

Sunday Express, Aug. 4th, 1946

" 'Let the troops read in bed,' says Montgomery. 'Then they'll be needing a few bedside lamps,' says I."

Sunday Express, Aug. 11th, 1946

"We're not going to run you in, chum—we'd just like to know how you do it."

Daily Express, Aug. 15th, 1946

"I don't mind 'em pinching our huts—it's this everlasting smell of kippers I can't stand."

Sunday Express, Aug. 18th, 1946

"I've a little surprise for you, George.   They let me bring Mummie, Auntie Ivy, Cousin Lil and Minnie."

Daily Express, Aug. 20th, 1946

"Let 'em get on with their milk strikes, that's what I say."

Daily Express, Aug. 23rd, 1946

"War, War, War—that's all you men think of."

Sunday Express, Aug. 25th, 1946

"Dear me, how time flies—football here already."

Daily Express, Aug. 31st, 1946

"Now I wonder which nasty horrid soldier wrote to Montgomery and complained that OUR sergeant won't let US read in bed?"

Seven Years Ago Today . . .

"I remember someone making a fool of himself galloping down the shelter with his gas mask on before Chamberlain had finished declaring war."

Daily Express, Sept. 3rd, 1946

"If this new fella ain't a member of my union, you can expect an unofficial strike from me any moment."

Daily Express, Sept. 6th, 1946

"It's me husband, Sir—he won't come out. Says he's had about all he can stand of the outside world."

Sunday Express, Sept. 8th, 1946

"I'm on a bike—what are you on?"

Daily Express, Sept. 10th, 1946

"I tell you I'm not a squatter—I've been to a sale and I *live* here."

Sunday Express, Sept. 15th, 1946

"No, we haven't a space ship ready yet—and if we had I fear we should have to draw the line at taking squatters to the moon."

Sunday Express, Sept. 22nd, 1946

—these bigger newspapers!

Daily Express, Sept. 24th, 1946

"These Russians! NO this—NO that—NO the other—and now NO war!"

Daily Express, Sept. 26th, 1946

"Ah well, my boy—nothin' for it but to go home and face some of your mother's cooking."

Daily Express, Oct. 10th, 1946

The old slogan comes back.

Sunday Express, Oct. 13th, 1946

"That's ten goals you've let through today—one more and we'll sell you to another team right cheap."

Sunday Express, Oct. 20th, 1946

"Bother the fuel-saving campaign."

Daily Express, Oct. 22nd, 1946

"Oh dear, I hope *he's* not going to start any trouble.'

"You'll have to mind your P's and Q's now that you've got this Morrison on your tracks."

Sunday Express, Nov. 3rd, 1946

"Late again? What's the matter—someone nobbled your 'orse?"

Daily Express, Nov. 14th, 1946

"Never saw a man so worried about losing his Christmas dinner."

Sunday Express, Nov. 17th, 1946.

"I don't suppose this weather helps the old police recruiting campaign much, do it, Fred?"

Daily Express, Nov. 19th, 1946

Snow has fallen in many districts. More is on the way.

Daily Express, Nov. 21st, 1946

"This go-slow strike'll shake the people who thought British railways couldn't go any slower."

Sunday Express, Nov. 24th, 1946

The Thames rises four inches and WHAM! away floats your pre-fab estate!

Daily Express, Nov. 28th, 1946

"And now here is a jolly quiz for everybody to join in. Have you all got your pencils and little pieces of paper ready?"

Sunday Express, Dec. 1st, 1946

"What was the name of that feller with a little moustache who couldn't stand people making jokes about 'im?"

Daily Express, Dec. 5th, 1946

"Effie, are you the one who's been telling the others not to go on unless the management recognise your union?"

Daily Express, Dec. 10th, 1946

"This year, gentlemen, all catapults, air guns, squeakers, buzzers and so forth will be deposited with me and returned to you AFTER the carol singing."

Sunday Express, Dec. 15th, 1946

"You say you were proceeding along the road whistling 'I'm Dreaming of a White Christmas' when these two gentlemen pounced upon you, causing grievous bodily harm."

Daily Express, Dec. 17th, 1946

"Excuse me! Any chance of fixing us up with a half bottle of whisky?"

Daily Express, Dec. 19th, 1946

"I've got one of them clever husbands I have—'Order a turkey from all of 'em,' he says, 'then we'll be sure of getting ONE,' says he."

Sunday Express, Dec. 22nd, 1946

"This ought to be handy for you—left unattended for three hours—no lights—and no number plates."

Daily Express, Dec. 24th, 1946

"Bright idea of yours—taking them to the circus—wasn't it?"

Sunday Express, Dec. 29th, 1946

"I broke all me Noo Year resolutions first day. Done yours yet, sir?"

Daily Express, Jan. 4th, 1947

"We know it's YOUR mine and all that—but the management would prefer fewer of these family inspections."

Sunday Express, Jan. 5th, 1947

"Just let any of me passengers come the old acid on our last day as clippies."

Daily Express, Jan. 9th, 1947

"Wouldn't surprise me if this was a put-up job—you all getting flu the same week as motor transport goes on strike."

Sunday Express, Jan. 12th, 1947

"Drat this new production drive—encouraging absenteeism, that's what it's doing."

Daily Express, Jan. 22nd, 1947

"There goes that funny Mr. Smith—got some idea about accepting the challenge, taking up the sword, speeding production and all that."

Daily Express, Jan. 24th, 1947

O the snow, the beautiful snow
Filling the sky and the earth below
Over the housetops, over the street,
Over the heads of the people you meet.

Dancing, flirting, skimming along,
Beautiful snow it can do nothing wrong.

—*from "Beautiful Snow",*
by John Whittaker Watson

Sunday Express, Jan. 26th, 1947

"Tractors replace horses—de-da, de-da, de-da . . ."

Daily Express, Jan. 30th, 1947

"George! Isn't it wonderful! Our new refrigerator's come at last!"

Sunday Express, Feb. 2nd, 1947

"Psst!—Nip in and ask your guv'nor if 'e could use a few logs."

Daily Express, Feb. 5th, 1947

"I'll laugh if there's no —— lines under this lot."

Daily Express, Feb. 6th, 1947

". . . and so, Mr. Shinwell, unless you send me an extra allocation of coal *immediately* I shall be compelled to close down my business."

Sunday Express, Feb. 9th, 1947

"I suppose *one* day someone'll have a crisis what the poor —— Pioneer Corps *don't* have to clear up."

Daily Express, Feb. 13th, 1947

"Turn out, boys—it's the chap again who bought that army flame-thrower to clear the snow off his garden path."

Sunday Express, Feb. 16th, 1947

"... in view of the excellent results achieved by this method during the crisis, the management has decided to abandon the use of electricity permanently."

Daily Express, Feb 18th, 1947

"What's the matter, chum—still cold?"

Daily Express, Feb. 20th, 1947

"I have received a report from the caretaker that a substantial quantity of coal disappeared from the school boiler house during the night."

Sunday Express, Feb. 23rd, 1947

DEPARTMENT OF ABSOLUTE FACT . . . "A change is almost certain in a day or two. And it's encouraging to know that something is going to happen, even if we don't know what it is . . ."—*Air Ministry Weather Report*

Daily Express, Feb. 26th, 1947

"Much of this and we'll all be like a lot of bloomin' owls."

Daily Express, Feb. 27th, 1947

"Well, how do the knights in shining armour struggling valiantly up the path to recovery like turning out at two in the morning?"

Sunday Express, Mar. 2nd, 1947

"You'll cop it—everybody's supposed to have gone back to work yesterday."

Daily Express, Mar. 4th, 1947

"O.K., here comes one of 'em."

Sunday Express, Mar. 9th, 1947

"Oh, everything's all right now—nothing to eat, no fire, no light—but the frost didn't get father's crocuses."

Daily Express, Mar. 12th, 1947

"Hurry up, Grandma, before the man comes and wants to know if we had a permit to build this lot."

Sunday Express, Mar. 16th, 1947

"Ah, well—there's always someone worse orf than yourself."

Daily Express, Mar. 18th, 1947

"The flowers that bloom in the spring, tra la . . ."

Sunday Express, Mar. 23rd, 1947

"The Sport of Kings—that's what they call it, m'dear."

Daily Express, Mar. 25th, 1947

"How does that story go about the little Dutch bloke who sat all night with his arm in a 'ole?"

Daily Express, Mar. 27th, 1947

"Beats me why anybody should *want* to bribe the B.B.C. to plug dance tunes."

Sunday Express, Mar. 30th, 1947

"I said, 'Oh to be in England now that April's here,' you old fool."

Daily Express, April 1st, 1947

"Nothing like a nice week-end at home to cheer us all up, eh chum?"

Daily Express, April 8th, 1947

Shop assistants who excel in civility and skill will be eligible for a "national certificate of retail efficiency."

Daily Express, April 10th, 1947

Spring comes to the great cities.
"How about me and you and a little pre-fab?"

Sunday Express, April 13th, 1947

"If Woodcock loses and Dalton pops on the taxes, these'll be a hot line tomorrow."

Daily Express, April 15th, 1947

"Never mind, dear, England's still got one hope—Gordon might win his Derby."

Daily Express, April 17th, 1947

"About time we had one of these sack-the-boss strikes."

Daily Express, April 24th, 1947

"Isn't that wonderful! From tomorrow we can have the wireless on all day long again."

Sunday Express, April 27th, 1947

"The sun never sets on the British Empire, do it?"

Daily Express, April 29th, 1947

"I've been trailing these Courtesy Cops all afternoon to see if they ever slip up."

Sunday Express, May 4th, 1947

"This 'Artley Shawcross says: 'The affairs of the country have too often been left to old, weary and disillusioned men and it's time youth took a hand.'"

Daily Express, May 6th, 1947

"I suppose it hasn't occurred to anybody that two years ago today father won the war for us."

Daily Express, May 8th, 1947

"Extremely bad taste, putting that there."

Sunday Express, May 11th, 1947

"We are worse than pagans. Dog-racing, prize-fighting, and other gambling are all evidence, etc., etc."
—*The Rev. F. C. Baker, St. Paul's Cathedral.*

Daily Express, May 13th, 1947

"There he goes—little old St. George hisself."

Sunday Express, May 18th, 1947

"What's up with you, inspired with the glorious incentive to work or did you find one of them stronger-beer pubs?"

Daily Express, May 20th, 1947

"This Whitsun his Lordship will be taking his own—er—'Staff of Life'."

Daily Express, May 22nd, 1947

"All right, chum—I know just what you're thinking."

Sunday Express, May 25th, 1947

"Looks like they made Nobby spend his Whitsun among the haunts of Fauna and Flora."

Daily Express, May 27th, 1947

"How much longer are they going to be working out this equal-pay-equal-work business?"

Sunday Express, June 1st, 1947

"Some of father's nice friends recommended this place—'LOVELY heat-wave here', they said."

Daily Express, June 5th, 1947

"Here we are, girls, 'tired, lack-lustre faces, waxy with too much starch and wistful for lack of proteins', says LOOK."

Daily Express, June 12th, 1947

"We'd have looked handy nipping around in this lot on D Day."

Sunday Express, June 15th, 1947

"Moths, Sir Edward, MOTHS!"

Daily Express, June 17th, 1947

"Making laws and passing 'em the same day! Don't give you time to think up a decent fiddle."

Daily Express, June 19th, 1947

"Be patient, Richard—they're only watching."

Sunday Express, June 22nd, 1947

"This Strachey-Cripps whisky allocation works out at about one tablespoon per adult per week.

Daily Express, June 24th, 1947

"They beat our boxers, they beat our 'orses, they beat us at tennis, but 'Itler couldn't beat our little old army."

Sunday Express, June 29th, 1947

"Useful sort, aren't you? Ten minutes to catch the train, and you lose the baby in this lot."

Daily Express, July 1st, 1947

"Ho! Off again? Who are we today—Dinny Pails? Mr. Kramer?"

Sunday Express, July 6th, 1947

"It'll break my heart if these Sunday bus strikes are going to stop me taking the wife and family out for the day."

Sunday Express, July 13th, 1947

"Don't take you long to turn a heat wave into a crime wave, do it?"

Daily Express, July 15th, 1947

"Is that the Direction of Labour into Industry Department? Well, about these six new heavy steel workers you've sent us . . ."

Daily Express, July 17th, 1947

"The sooner you forget the N.W. Frontier and remember you're in N.W.11, the sooner I'll like it."

Daily Express, July 22nd, 1947

"It says here that when your teacher explained that the Nations of the World were striving in unity towards a glorious Peace, you emitted a long, low rumbling noise resembling the sound 'Burrrrrrrp'."

Daily Express, July 24th, 1947

"Watch out for that wicket-keeper—just as you're going to swipe the ball he'll ask you what you're doing here instead of working to speed production or something."

Sunday Express, July 27th, 1947

WHAT IS THE LOVELIEST AGE OF A BABY?

0—6 MONTHS:

"Isn't-he-like-his-father?" age.

6—12 MONTHS:

"Isn't-he-like-his-mother?" age.

12—18 MONTHS:

"I-think-he's-like-his-father-after-all" age.

18 MONTHS—2 YEARS:

"He's-just-getting-interesting" age.

5—8 YEARS:

"Georgie's-getting-on-awfully-well-at-school" age.

8—30 YEARS:

"Chalking - on - pavement - rude - words - on - the - side - of - your - car - window - breaking - arson - and-general-chaos" age.

Daily Express, July 29th, 1947

"My dad says it's easy to see who gets most of the rations in SOMEBODY'S family."

Daily Express, July 31st, 1947

"Miss Emily, what is this I hear about a Spiv tossing you double or quits for the takings and you losing?"

Sunday Express, Aug. 3rd, 1947

"Here comes the first lot back to work—strainin' like grey'arnds at the leash."

Daily Express, Aug. 5th, 1947

"It's a bit late to keep telling Father you've known all along he'd have to pull his socks up sooner or later."

Sunday Express, Aug. 10th, 1947

"I suppose one could go on indefinitely making little jokes about the Grouse season REALLY starting after last week's crisis announcements."
—(*Grouse shooting officially starts today.*)

Daily Express, Aug. 12th, 1947

"Wouldn't surprise me if that Cecil de Mille or someone don't drop a few atom bombs on us for this."

Daily Express, Aug. 14th, 1947

"When you've finished discussing all this lovely machinery we're going to have in a few years' time, could you fetch me another piece of string?"

Sunday Express, Aug. 24th, 1947

"Even if they do make you and father boiler-makers' mates or something, Godfrey, you might *like* it after all."

Sunday Express, Aug. 31st, 1947

"If they give an 11-hour day and a 4-day week, I suppose that means we're going to have everybody at home for a 24-hour day 3 days a week."

Daily Express, Sept. 2nd, 1947

" 'Eels and butterflies' sounds MUCH nicer than 'Spivs and Drones' don't it?"

Daily Express, Sept. 4th, 1947

"You can start thinking of El Alamein, D Day, and the rest of 'em as sports outings—in future you'll be keeping order at the Housewives' League."

Sunday Express, Sept. 14th, 1947

" 'You start next week as stoker in a hot-pie factory,' he said. 'And you can go to a hotter place than that,' said I."

Sunday Express, Sept. 21st, 1947

"Marked increase in the size of congregations these days, Vicar."

Daily Express, Sept. 23rd, 1947

"Well, you can't take Margaret Lockwood or Pat Roc, so come on!"

Daily Express, Sept. 25th, 1947

"Hey, Dad—remember those last two gallons of petrol you hid in the garage . . ."

Daily Express, Sept. 30th, 1947

"Says they wouldn't let him have any 'E' coupons."

Daily Express, Oct. 16th, 1947

"Looks like somebody else is hibernating this year."

Sunday Express, Oct. 26th, 1947

Ho! Mother was going to have a new hat, everybody was going to have new boots—if father's cert had won the Cambridgeshire.

Daily Express, Oct. 30th, 1947

"Seems like this one does not wish to sell his cattle to the Black Market."

Sunday Express, Nov. 2nd, 1947

"What's this we hear about you taking bets that the Russians and Americans will have a go by Christmas?"

Daily Express, Oct. 14th, 1947